THE MARATHON

Hadyn Middleton
Illustrated by Cheryl Cook

Rigby®

A Harcourt Achieve Imprint

www.Rigby.com
1-800-531-5015

Literacy by Design Leveled Readers: *The Marathon*

ISBN-13: 978-1-4189-3786-7
ISBN-10: 1-4189-3786-X

Printed in China
1B 2 3 4 5 6 7 8 985 13 12 11 10 09 08 07

Contents

Chapter 1

Nate's Big Announcement

At dinner Nate shared some exciting news. "I'm running in the town marathon. The race is in two months, and I plan to win it!"

"Oh, wow!" cried his little sister Maya. "I'd like to run in that race, too!"

"Maya," laughed Nate, "do you even know how long a marathon is?"

Maya had no idea, but Mom piped up, "It's like twenty miles, right?"

"No," said Nate, "it's 26 miles, 385 yards. Even in your dreams you couldn't run that far, Maya!"

"And anyway," Nate went on, "kids under 18 years old aren't allowed to run such a long distance because their bodies just can't stand up to all the pressure. My older body, however, is able to meet the marathon challenge. Or it will be by the time I've completed the really tough training program I've made for myself."

"Well, can I help you train then?" asked Maya. "Or am I too young to be your coach as well?"

Nate shook his head and said, "Thanks, Maya, but there's really nothing for a coach to help me with. All I have to do is get myself into shape to run those miles and yards faster than anyone else. It's not rocket science."

All that week after work, Nate went running at the local track, while Maya rode her bike round and round watching him. It seemed like a weird distance for a race to go 26 miles, 385 yards. Maya wondered why it was that long and why it was called a *marathon*. The next day she checked out a book about marathons from the library.

"Listen to this," said Maya before dinner. She opened her book and read, "More than 2,000 years ago, the Greeks beat the Persians in a battle at a city called Marathon. Afterward, a soldier ran more than 20 miles to the Greek city of Athens with the good news. When the modern Olympic Games began in 1896 in Greece, the organizers included a long road race that was the same distance as his journey and called it the marathon."

Everything You Need to Know About the MARATHON

"Nice facts, Maya," said Nate, "but that's history, and the only marathon that I'm interested in is the one I'm going to win! Running sure makes me hungry, so what's for dinner, Mom?"

"We're having burgers and fries, with ice cream for dessert," Mom answered.

"He needs healthier food that's good for him," Maya said.

"Why is that?" asked Mom.

"This book says a healthy diet is important for marathon runners. Food gives your body energy so it works properly. Different foods give you different energy levels. Marathon runners need foods high in carbohydrates—foods like pasta, bread, potatoes, and fruits such as bananas."

Mom listened to what Maya said, and week by week the family's meals got healthier, which secretly pleased Maya. She liked pasta and potatoes. She was also interested in learning how important it was for athletes to eat right.

"Carbohydrates are good because they're easy to digest," Maya read, "and they easily turn into energy-giving glucose—a kind of sugar that is found in the blood. It also turns into glycogen, which is an important source of energy for the liver and muscles."

"Is that a fact?" asked Nate. "All I know is I'm *always* hungry now!"

"That's because you're burning off so many calories through exercising," Maya explained.

Chapter 2

A Perfect Working Machine

After a month of training, Nate looked really fit. "My body is a perfect working machine," he purred with pride after a long run.

"Thanks to all your aerobic activity," said Maya.

"*Aerobic* activity?" asked Nate.

"Aerobic means using oxygen to produce energy you need. When you breathe in oxygen from the air," Maya explained, "it goes into your lungs, and is pumped to your muscles. Why don't you do some strength training, too? Using weights will toughen up the muscles around your heart, so more blood will be pumped to your muscles."

Nate agreed that was a good idea, so he started lifting weights after work. He also went for longer and longer runs.

"Will you have to run through the woods during the race?" asked Maya as she followed him on her bike.

"I'm not sure," gasped Nate. "I just like the scenery better out here!"

After the run that afternoon, Nate said, "If you *really* want to lend me a hand, you could carry my drink bottle in your bike basket. Running makes me so thirsty, but the water's heavy to carry."

"You got it," cried Maya, "and can I carry your water for you on the day of the race, too?"

"There will be drink stations along the route," Nate answered, "so that we can pick up cups of water as we race past. That's something else to practice—drinking out of a cup while I'm racing along the road. I'm sure it's not as easy as it looks!"

"What would happen if you *didn't* drink while you ran?" Maya asked during Nate's next long run.

"I'd get really, *really* thirsty," laughed Nate.

"Is that all that would happen?" asked Maya.

"I don't know," shrugged Nate, "but I guess you're going to look up the facts in your book and tell me, right?"

Maya was astonished at what the book told her. She had always imagined that under their skins, people were made of nothing except muscles and bone, but she learned that water makes up about 60 percent of a person's body. She shook her arm back and forth, then listened for water sloshing around inside! (She didn't hear any.)

"Water helps stop the body from overheating," she told Nate and Mom later. "For a body to work in a healthy way, it has to stay at a temperature between 98 and 100 degrees Fahrenheit. When you run, your muscles produce extra heat, so the body handles this rise in temperature by sweating. As this sweat dries on your skin, you lose heat, and your body cools down."

"What would happen," Maya wondered, "if you ran out of sweat?"

The book told her this could be a major problem for long-distance runners, especially in hot weather. She read that a runner might lose about three and one-half pints of sweat in a single hour. This fluid had to be replaced, and that was done by drinking water. Otherwise, the runner would get dried out, thirsty, and weak. This is called getting dehydrated, and that would be no fun at all.

Dehydration could cause sickness, breathing difficulties, and even heat stroke. The book said that, when you are training or running in a race, the best thing to do is to keep drinking small amounts of water often.

"In that case," thought Maya, "I just might take along some extra water for Nate on the big day."

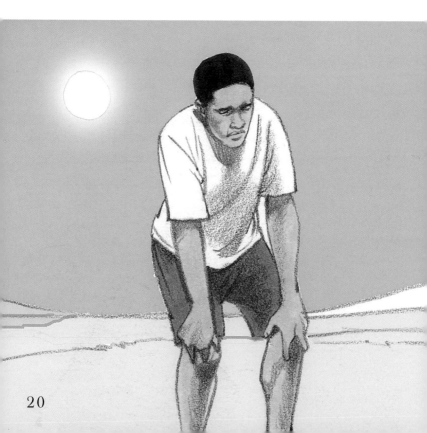

Chapter 3

Exhausted!

Just three weeks before the race, something started to go wrong. "I don't know what's up," Nate complained, "but I feel so weak and tired that I don't think I can run even one mile today, and I had planned to do twenty miles. I thought training was meant to make you *more* fit!"

"You haven't been resting enough," Maya said, waving the book at him. "When you train, lots of your body's parts, such as tiny bits of muscle, break down so that they can then rebuild themselves more strongly. However, you need to be resting for this rebuilding to happen, and you keep training *all* the time. . ."

But Nate was only half-listening because he was falling asleep.

From that day on, Nate made sure
he took regular rest days in his training
program, and he never felt so weak or tired
again.

"I don't know what Nate would do
without your helpful hints, Maya," said
Mom. "I hope he's thanking you for all
your coaching tips."

Maya laughed, "Nate never thanks me for anything!"

"Just you wait and see. He certainly will if he does well in his race next week, and if he doesn't, then I'll tell him that he can cook all his own healthy meals in the future!" Mom chuckled.

Chapter 4
The Big Day

The day of the town marathon finally arrived, and Maya jumped out of bed and opened the curtains to find a hot sun beating down.

"Hmm," she thought, "Nate will sweat like crazy on such a hot day, so I'll *definitely* have to take some extra water along, just in case he needs water between drink stations."

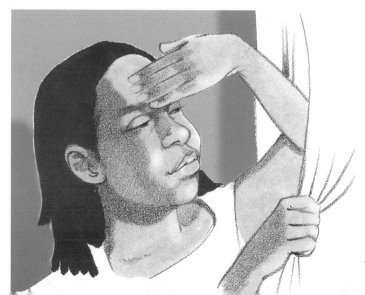

After breakfast Maya helped Nate pack his big race bag. "Don't forget this," she said, handing him a huge, folded-up sheet of tin foil.

"What's that for?" asked Nate.

"To wrap yourself in when you've finished running, or else you might cool down too fast, and then you might faint."

"Is that a fact?" grinned Nate.

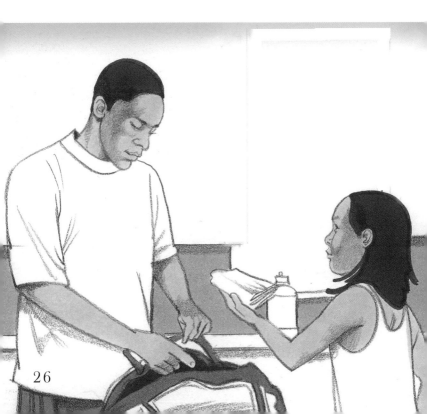

Many runners set off from the starting
point downtown. The route would be a
great big loop to the outer part of town,
into the fields and hills, and then back
around into town again. Nate, wearing
his red running shirt and his lucky green
baseball hat, got a great start. In fact, it
looked like he had taken an early lead.

Mom had agreed to ride with Maya as she followed Nate's run. They pedaled as hard as they could, but it wasn't easy for them to keep up with the runners. Some of the people watching kept getting in their way, and sometimes the runners went down streets where no traffic was allowed, including Maya and Mom on their bikes. Even before the runners ran out of town, they had completely lost sight of Nate.

As they passed each drink station, Maya asked the race officials if they had seen a runner in a red shirt and green baseball hat.

"Yes, he was way out in front when he passed here!" said officials at the first three stations. "He was running so fast that he didn't even stop to grab a drink!"

"Hmm," thought Maya, "that doesn't sound good."

A short time later, Mom and Maya hit the section of the race route that took them out of town and into the fields. The lady at the next drink station said no one at all had run past yet.

"But my brother *must* have!" cried Maya. "Back at the last station he was in the lead, and we've ridden along the route since then."

"Maybe he took a wrong turn somewhere," said Mom, sounding very worried.

DRINKING

"Oh, poor Nate!" thought Maya. What if he had gone down the wrong road? After all that hard work he'd put into preparing himself for the big day, she hoped he didn't run into such bad luck!

The signs marking the route *were* sometimes a little unclear. "I have to go find him," Maya told herself, "and fast!"

Turning their bikes around, Mom and Maya furiously pedaled back to a fork in the road. *Surely* Nate couldn't have turned left and not right! The left-hand road led straight uphill into some thick forest, but where else could he be? They zoomed up the hill and in among the evergreen trees, where they started to call out Nate's name.

Round and round Mom and Maya rode—first on the road, then on narrow paths leading into the woods. "Nate! Nate!" Mom called out. "Are you lost in here somewhere?"

Then to Maya's horror she saw that he was! A glimpse of his red shirt led Maya to a small clearing where Nate was kneeling on the ground, panting, gasping, and unable to speak.

"Nate!" cried Maya, rushing to his aid and knowing exactly what had happened. He had been running for too long without drinking anything, so now he was dehydrated.

"I have just the thing you need," said Maya. "Look, I've got some water! Drink this and soon you'll be back on your feet."

Nate had been so far ahead when he took the wrong turn, only five runners had caught up to him. With Mom and Maya cheering him on, he ran his hardest and was almost in the lead again.

"There's just one runner in front of you now," Maya said as they passed the last drink station. "You can do this, Nate. You can do it!"

Nate gulped down one last cupful of water, which reminded Maya of a race car being topped off with gas for the last few laps of the race. Minutes later, he flew past the runner up ahead. Then he raced across the finish line to become the town's marathon champion!

FINISH LINE

Maya gave Nate a hug, unfolded the foil sheet, and wrapped him up in it snugly. Mom kissed her children with pride, and then made a serious face. "Now tell me, Maya," she said, "has Nate thanked you for all the help you've given him?"

"Thank you, thank you!" panted Nate before Maya could answer. "You're the best coach in the whole history of the marathon, and that's a fact!"

Later that night Nate, Maya, and Mom all enjoyed a big dinner of lasagna, salad, and garlic bread with a tall, cold glass of milk to wash it all down.

"That's enough running for me for a while," Nate said. "I'm taking a break next week!"

Maya and Mom laughed and agreed that was a good idea!